For Patrick – *A.K.*
For Adrienne – *J.W.*

Bumblebee copyright © Frances Lincoln Limited 2011
Text copyright © J.V. Wilson 2011
Illustrations copyright ©Adrienne Kennaway 2011

First published in Great Britain and the USA in 2011 by
Frances Lincoln Children's Books, 4 Torriano Mews,
Torriano Avenue, London NW5 2RZ
www.franceslincoln.com

The author would like to thank Dr Tomás Murray of the Crops Research Centre in Carlow,
County Carlow, Ireland for his invaluable assistance.

A catalogue record for this book is available from the British Library.

ISBN 978-1-84780-008-4

Illustrated with watercolours

Set in Palatino

Printed in Shenzhen, Guangdong, China by WKT Co. Ltd. in November 2010

1 3 5 7 9 8 6 4 2

Bumblebee

J.V. Wilson

Adrienne Kennaway

FRANCES LINCOLN
CHILDREN'S BOOKS

It is the first day of spring, and a sleepy bumblebee queen flies out to find food and a nest. Throughout the cold winter she has slept alone in an old, dry mouse-hole beneath the ground, and now she has woken up with a single goal – to build her own colony for the year.

The bumblebee queen visits dandelion and pussy-willow flowers, where she drinks nectar and collects pollen by brushing her hairy body over the flowers.

She never wastes any food. Before leaving the flower, she collects extra nectar in a special honey stomach in her belly and, using her front legs, packs any extra pollen into baskets on her back legs. This will feed her future family.

With her belly full of nectar and both back legs loaded with pollen, the bumblebee queen flies low to the ground searching for a suitable nest. As she goes, she buzzes around a young stag and a crouching fox.

While gathering food, the bumblebee queen has been pollinating flowers by passing the pollen on her body from flower to flower. This allows the flowers to produce seeds for new flowers next year.

At last she finds an old, dry mouse-hole – perfect for starting a new colony.

It is dusk, and the bumblebee queen
has been flying since the early morning.
Now she builds her first honey-pot at
the entrance to her nest.

Then, by mixing nectar and pollen together, she makes a lump of bee bread, on which she lays the first eggs of the year.

To keep her eggs warm and dry, she covers them with a sheet of bees' wax produced from eight special holes under her belly.

Like a bird, the bumblebee queen sits on her eggs to keep them warm during the cold spring nights, until they hatch into tiny white larvae. Within weeks the larvae have spun a silky case, called a cocoon, around themselves and the queen covers them with an extra layer of wax.

It is not long before the shaky young worker bees have eaten their way out of their cocoons, ready to help the queen with her tasks. The empty wax they emerge from is reused to store extra honey and pollen.

As summer arrives, the nest becomes busy. Early one evening a curious weasel pokes its head down the mouse-hole. The buzzing of the worker bees creates a roar in the entrance tunnel. The weasel doesn't stay long!

Later, a digging sound outside the mouse-hole brings some workers flying out to protect their nest – straight into a startled badger. The badger leaves in a hurry, too!

Then the trickiest invader of all flies into the nest –
a cuckoo bee. Although she looks like a bumblebee,
she cannot produce workers or start a colony of her
own. She plans to get rid of the bumblebee queen
and use the nest and workers to raise cuckoo bees.
Since she smells rather like the bumblebee queen
she can sneak in and hide in a dark corner.

But she is unlucky. The workers smell her disguise,
and she is driven out.

The bumblebee nest is now well established. Its stores are full of honey and pollen. The queen has laid more eggs which will produce new queen bees and male drones.

The new males are the first to emerge, but they are very lazy and get in everyone's way, so they are soon thrown out by the busy worker bees! Outside, they feed on pollen and nectar, getting ready to mate as soon as the new queen bees leave the hive.

On a late summer's day, the old bumblebee queen flies out of her wonderful nest for the last time. She drinks some heather nectar with her long tongue and is happy with her year's work.

Finally, as autumn comes, the new bumblebee queens
emerge from their silky cocoons and leave their nest in
the old mouse-hole to mate with the male drones outside.

Once mated, each young bumblebee queen flies low to
the ground, searching for a safe place to sleep until spring,
when she will go off and start a whole new colony.

Helping bumblebees

Bumblebees are having a difficult time in many parts of the world. We're not sure whether it's destruction of bees' habitat, pesticides, disease or something else that is affecting them, but whatever it is, bees are disappearing in large numbers. This is a problem because we need bumblebees to pollinate our crops and fruit trees.

One of the best ways to help bees is by planting traditional cottage-garden flowers and wildflowers which are full of nectar and pollen. Here are some flowers, bushes and trees that bees love, listed under the seasons when they flower:

Spring	Early summer	Late summer
Apple tree	Chives	Bramble
Bluebell	Forgetmenot	Buddleia
Cherry tree	Foxglove	Catmint
Flowering currant	Fuschia	Cornflower
Pear tree	Geranium	Hollyhock
Plum tree	Heather	Lavender
Red dead-nettle	Honeysuckle	Marjoram
Rosemary	Poppy	Mint
White dead-nettle	Raspberry	Red clover
Willow trees and shrubs	Sage	Snapdragon
	Thyme	Sunflower
	Veronica	Viper's bugloss
	White clover	
	Wisteria	

Other things you can do to help bees:
• Let the grass in your garden grow longer to encourage clover and wild flowers to grow.
• Make a woodpile out of logs and dead branches in a shady corner of your garden. Leave it to rot, so that bees can hibernate there during the winter.
• Don't disturb any bees which want to spend the winter in your garden shed.

Visit www.bumblebeeconservation.org.uk

Glossary

bee bread   pollen moistened with nectar. It is stored to feed the first batch of worker bees.

bumblebee   a bee from the Bombus family. Its relative the honeybee is from the Apis family.

cocoon   the layer of silk spun by a larva when it is ready to change into an adult insect.

colony   a group of bees living together in a nest (not in a man-made hive).

cuckoo bee   a bee from the Psithyrus family. It cannot start a colony or produce workers. Instead, it takes over existing nests, kills the queen and uses her workers to rear new queen and male drone cuckoo bees.

drone   a male bee. All workers and queens are female.

honey stomach   a place in the bee's gut for storing nectar.

larvae   a bit like butterfly caterpillars. Bee larvae are fed by adult bees.

nectar   a sugar-rich liquid produced by flowers to encourage pollination by insects.

pollen   the powder produced by the male parts of a flower.

pollination   transferring pollen from the male parts to the female parts of a flower to begin the production of seeds.

queen   a female bee which lays both male and female eggs and stops other bees in the nest from reproducing. Bumble queens live for one year.

worker   a female bee that does most of the work in a colony: nursing, cleaning, defending the nest and foraging for food. She rarely lays eggs, but when she does, they are only male eggs. She lives for about six weeks.